Romeo, Romeo

Peter Leigh

Published in association with
The Basic Skills Agency

Hodder & Stoughton

A MEMBER OF THE HODDER HEADLINE GROUP

Acknowledgements
Cover: Lee Montgomery
Illustrations: Jo Blake

Orders: please contact Bookpoint Ltd, 130 Milton Park, Abingdon, Oxon OX14 4SB. Telephone: (44) 01235 827720, Fax: (44) 01235 400454. Lines are open from 9.00–6.00, Monday to Saturday, with a 24 hour message answering service. Email address: orders@bookpoint.co.uk

British Library Cataloguing in Publication Data
A catalogue record for this title is available from The British Library

ISBN 0 340 80078 X

First published 2001
Impression number   10 9 8 7 6 5 4 3 2
Year   2007 2006 2005 2004 2003 2002 2001

Copyright © 2001 Peter Leigh

All rights reserved. No part of this publication may be reproduced or transmitted in any form or by any means, electronic or mechanical, including photocopying, recording, or any information storage and retrieval system, without permission in writing from the publisher or under licence from the Copyright Licensing Agency Limited. Further details of such licences (for reprographic reproduction) may be obtained from the Copyright Licensing Agency Limited, of 90 Tottenham Court Road, London W1P 9HE.

Typeset by SX Composing DTP, Rayleigh, Essex.
Printed in Great Britain for Hodder & Stoughton Educational, a division of Hodder Headline Plc, 338 Euston Road, London NW1 3BH by Athanaeum Press, Gateshead, Tyne & Wear.

About the play

It's drama!
The teacher has told the class to read **Romeo and Juliet**.

The Class

- **Becki**
- **Kate**
- **Jaz**
- **Seth**
- **Tom**

Seth What have we got to do, then?
Jaz Miss said we had to do a bit from *Romeo and Juliet*.
Seth Can't we do something else?
I want to do a fight.
Tom There's a fight at the beginning of *Romeo and Juliet*.
Seth Great! Let's do that.
You and me can do the fight, Tom.

He pretends to shoot

'Eat lead, you mothers! Pow! Pow!'
Kate You're just going to mess about.
Let's do a more interesting bit.
Becki Let's do a love scene.
Kate Yes, that's better. It's more grown-up.
Seth I don't want to do a stupid girly bit.
Let's do the fight at the start.
Jaz We've got to choose a bit we all like, and then do it together.
Seth Well, I'm not doing a stupid love scene.
Becki And I'm not doing a stupid fight.

Tom	Why don't we all do a bit each?
Seth	Good idea. Let's start with the fight. Ker-bam! Zappa-zappa-zappa!
Tom	Is that all right with you, Becki?
Becki	I suppose so!
Jaz	Right then, we'll do the fight.
Seth	Great! I'm the hard man. What's he called?
Jaz	Tybalt.
Seth	Right, that's me. Who's the other one?
Jaz	Benvolio.
Seth	Right! Tom! You're Ben what's-his-name. Stand over there.

He pushes Tom to the end of the room.

Right, we're ready.
Everyone watching? OK! Let's go!

He rushes across to Tom

'You're finished, Ben!
You're dead meat, Ben!
You hear what I'm saying, Ben!
I'm gonna . . .'

He realises that everyone is staring at him.

What? What's the matter?

Jaz	What was that?
Seth	The fight at the beginning, with Ben.
	What do you think it was?
Kate	What about the words?
Seth	What words?
Kate	Shakespeare's words.
	You've got to use Shakespeare's words.
Seth	I'm not using his words. They're rubbish.
	Mine are much better.
Jaz	Look! You've got to use his words.
	Otherwise there's no point doing it.
Kate	There's no point in any case.
Becki	Too right! This is stupid.
Jaz	All right, all right!
	Well, are you going to use his words?
Seth	Do I have to?
Jaz	Yes!
Seth	(*grumbling*) Oh, all right, then.
	What words does he say?
Tom	(*looks in the book*)
	'I bite my thumb at thee!'
Seth	Is that it?

Tom   Yes – well there's a bit more,
          but that's what the fight's about.
Seth   Oh great!
          'I bite my thumb at thee!'
          That's really going to scare them.
          All these hard men, these Capulets,
          all ready to cane you
          and what do you say?
          'I bite my thumb at thee!'
          They're really going to run away at that!

Jaz	Look, it's just an insult, that's all.
Seth	No, it's not.
	I wouldn't care if anyone said that to me.
Jaz	It's just the same as giving the finger.
Tom	What about when that little kid
	gave you the finger?
	You chased him half-way round
	the school.
Jaz	That's right.
Tom	And you never caught him.
Seth	Well, that's different, isn't it?
Jaz	No it isn't –
	giving a finger and biting your thumb
	are exactly the same thing
	only four hundred years apart.
Tom	Perhaps in another four hundred years
	we'll do something different –
	like waggling your ears or something.
Jaz	That'll be good – 'I waggle my ears at thee!'
Seth	Yes, you'd be good at that
	with ears like yours.
Jaz	Oh, very funny!
Kate	Oh, this is stupid!
	It's always the same with you boys –
	you always end up having
	silly arguments.

Becki	Just like in the play.
Kate	That's right.
	I mean, who cares what gang you're in.
	It's only little boys playing with swords.
Jaz	Look, we're never going to get anywhere like this.
Kate	Let's do another bit.
	You boys can do the fight later on.
Becki	(*looking in the book*)
	Who's this 'Nurse' then?
	Is it a hospital? Are there any doctors?
Kate	No, it's not that sort of nurse.
	I read it in the notes. It's a wet-nurse.
Jaz	What's a wet-nurse?
Kate	You know, for babies.
Jaz	I don't know.
	What do you mean 'for babies'?
Kate	When a woman didn't want
	to feed a baby herself,
	she gave it to another woman
	to feed it for her.
Jaz	What? Breast-feed?
Kate	Yes.
Jaz	Oh that's disgusting, that is,
	breast-feeding someone else's baby.

Kate	Well, that's what they did all the time in those days. Look it says here, her daughter was the same age as Juliet but she died, so she fed Juliet instead.
Tom	Look, are we going to do some drama, or just sit around and chat.
Jaz	You're right. Let's do something.
Kate	Let's do the bit where Romeo meets Juliet.
Jaz	Good idea. Who's going to be Juliet?
Becki	Oh, me please. I've always wanted to be an actress.
Jaz	All right then. What about Romeo?

Silence

You were all keen enough a moment ago.

Seth	I'm not going to read that – it's soft.
Kate	Don't be silly. It's only acting.

Still silence

Jaz All right then. I'll do it myself.

He reads slowly.

> 'If I pro-fane with my un-worth-i-est hand
> This holy shrine, the gentle sin is this –
> My lips two blushing pilgrims
>   ready stand
> To smooth that rough touch with
>   a gentle kiss.'

Tom What does that mean?
Jaz I don't know. I just read it.
Tom What does 'profane' mean?
Kate It means 'make dirty'.
That's it. He must be holding her hands.
So he says if his hands are
too rough and dirty,
his lips are ready to kiss it better.
Becki Oh, that's nice.
Tom But what about the rest of it –
the 'holy shrine' and the 'blushing pilgrims'?
Kate Well, he's saying she's like a saint,
and his lips are pilgrims
come to worship her.
Seth Why does he say all that?
Why doesn't he just get on with it?
Becki That's just typical of you. You're so crude.

Kate	He's trying to chat her up.
	He's spinning her a line.
Seth	But no-one would say that. It's stupid.
Becki	What would you say,
	if you're such an expert.
Seth	Well, I wouldn't call a girl a saint.
	And I wouldn't worship her.
	Especially the girls round here.
Becki	Why not? What's wrong with that?
	You ought to listen to this Romeo.
	You could learn something.
	I think it's quite sexy, myself.
Kate	Good for you, Becki. So do I.
	Go on, it's your turn now.
	What does Juliet say?
Becki	*takes a deep breath, and reads slowly*
	'Good pilgrim, you do wrong your hand too much,
	Which manner-ly devo-tion shows in this.
	For saints have hands that pilgrims' hands do touch,
	And palm to palm is holy palmers kiss.'
Seth	Well, what does that mean, then?
Tom	She's telling him to get lost.

Seth	Why doesn't she just tell him
	if she doesn't like him,
	instead of all those words?
Jaz	She does like him. That's the point.
	She's playing hard to get. All girls do that.
Kate	No they don't.
Jaz	Yes they do.
	If a girl really likes a boy
	she always plays hard to get
	just to egg him on.
Seth	Is that true?
Jaz	Yes, of course.
Kate	No, it's not. Don't listen to him.
Seth	So, all those girls that say 'No'
	when I ask them out –
	does that mean they really like me?
	They're just playing hard to get.

Everyone laughs.

Becki	Oh never mind, Seth.
	Keep trying – you'll get there in the end.
	Just listen to Romeo.
	He's got what it takes.
	Juliet's not playing very hard to get.

Kate	No, but they *are* playing,
	except it's more like tennis.
Seth	What? Like tennis?
Kate	Yes. They're knocking the ball
	backwards and forwards over the net.
	Look, Romeo serves to Juliet –
	he calls her a saint, and goes to kiss her.
	Fifteen-love to Romeo.
	Juliet stops him
	and says if she really were a saint
	he should kiss her palm to palm –
	that's the right way to treat saints.
	Fifteen-all.
Tom	And what does Romeo say?
Jaz	'Have not saints lips, and holy palmers too?'
Seth	He wants to get his lips going, doesn't he?
Kate	Right!
	So that's thirty-fifteen to Romeo,
	and Juliet says . . .
Becki	'Ay pilgrim, lips that they must use in prayer.'

Kate	So she's stopped him again.
	Thirty-all!
	And he knocks it back to her . . .
Jaz	'O then dear saint, let lips do what hands do.
	They pray; grant thou, lest faith turn to despair.'
Kate	That's a good one.
	Forty-thirty to Romeo.
	She can only just get it back . . .
Becki	'Saints do not move, though grant for prayers' sake.'

Kate	Deuce! But Romeo can't be stopped.
	He moves in with a killer smash ...
Jaz	'Then move not, while my prayer's
	effect I take.'
Kate	And he kisses her.
Seth	Yes! Game, set and match to Romeo!
Kate	Well, it took some doing,
	but he got there in the end.
Seth	Well, go on then.
Jaz	Go on what?
Seth	Kiss her.
Jaz	I'm not kissing her.
Seth	Yes, you are.
	You're playing Romeo,
	and it says 'he kisses her' –
	so go on, kiss her.
Becki	I'm not having him kiss me.
Seth	It's acting, isn't it?
	You said you wanted to be an actress,
	so go on, act.
Becki	*she hesitates, then ...*
	Oh, all right then!

... and gives him a quick peck on the cheek.

Seth	She did it!
	He won't wash for a week now,
	will you, Jaz?
Jaz	Oh shut up.
Seth	Not much feeling, though, was there?
	Can't you put a bit more into it?
Jaz	Look! We've done it! All right?
	Let's move on.
Tom	What shall we do now?
	What happens in the rest of the play?
Kate	They get married, I think.
Jaz	They get married? But she's only fourteen.
Seth	Fourteen?
	Did you say Juliet is only fourteen?
Kate	That's right.
	It says so somewhere.
Seth	That's a bit young, isn't it?
	To be getting married and everything?
Becki	If you meet the right boy,
	age doesn't matter.
	My cousin's engaged to this boy,
	and she's only fourteen.
Seth	How old's the boy?

Becki Twenty-eight.
Jaz Twenty-eight?
That's not a boy, that's an old man.
Seth A dirty old man, by the sound of it.
Becki Yes, well, maybe he is a bit old.
In fact, I think she only got engaged
so she could flash the ring around.
Tom What did her mum and dad say
when she told them?
Becki They went mad!
Kate I think mine would too.
Tom What do Juliet's mum and dad think
about it?
Kate They're all for it.
They want her to get married.
Except not to Romeo.
They've arranged a husband for her.
Jaz That's sick, that is –
the parents arranging the marriage.
Becki Oh, I don't know.
A lot of people have arranged marriages,
and it seems to work out all right.
Stops you making any mistakes.

Jaz	I'll make my own mistakes thank you very much. Besides, who says you've got to get married in any case?
Kate	That's right, especially if no-one wants to marry you in the first place, which is true in your case.
Jaz	Oh, very funny!
Kate	No, you're right. I was only joking. Parents shouldn't interfere. It's your life.
Seth	My parents have made a real mess of their lives. Why should they tell me how to live mine?
Tom	Perhaps it's because they've made such a mess – they don't want you to make the same mistakes.
Becki	Tom's right! Parents are bound to interfere if they care about you. It's only the ones that don't care that leave you alone.
Kate	But look at what Juliet's dad actually says.
Becki	What do you mean?

Kate	Well, she tells him
	she doesn't want to marry
	the man he wants.
	And look what he calls her–
	'you green-sickness carrion,
	you baggage, you tallow-face!'
Becki	What does that mean?
Kate	I don't know exactly,
	but it's not very nice, is it?
	He's not exactly the kind, understanding
	dad, is he?
	'Get thee to church,' he says,
	'or never after look me in the face.'
	So he's really saying,
	'Do what I want, or get out!'
Seth	That sounds just like my Dad.
	Never mind all this 'understanding' stuff.
Kate	Yes, but look how it ends –
	in the death of his only daughter.
Tom	Is that what happens in the end?
Kate	Yes, they all get killed.
Becki	Oh, that's sad.

Seth	Great! Let's do that bit, where they all get killed. Is there a big fight?
Kate	No, Romeo drinks poison.
Seth	I can do that. *He holds his throat, coughing.* Eurrgh . . . eurrgh . . . *He falls across the desk, and chokes out . . .* Tell Juliet . . . I did it . . . for her! *. . . and dies!* **Jaz** *and* **Tom** *applaud.*

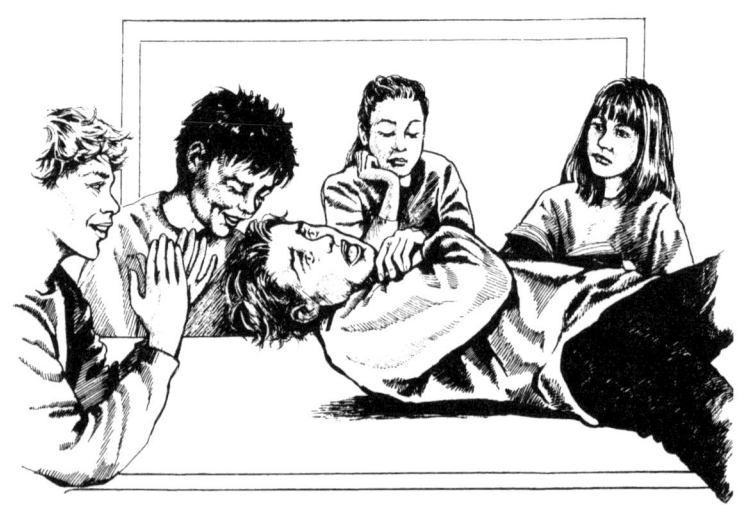

Seth Thank you, fans!
Kate The trouble is,
you've got to read all this as well.

She points to a page in the book.

Seth What? I'm not reading all that.
I'm just doing the dying, that's all.
Becki Let's not do a death bit. That's sad.
Let's do a famous bit.
Let's do the balcony scene.
Kate Yes, let's.
You carry on with Juliet, Becki.
You're doing really well. Come on Jaz!
Jaz I'm not reading anymore.
Can't someone else do it?
What about you, Tom?
The others Yes, come on Tom. You can do it.
Tom Oh, all right. But don't laugh.

He takes a deep breath.

'But soft! What light . . .'
Jaz But what?
Tom 'But soft'!
Jaz What does that mean?

Seth	It's American for 'bum'.
	It means Juliet's got a soft bum.
Kate	Don't be stupid. It doesn't mean that at all.
Seth	It should do.
	That would be more interesting.
Kate	Let's just get on, shall we? Carry on, Tom.
Tom	'But soft, what light through
	yonder window breaks.
	It is the east, and Juliet is the sun . . .'
Seth	Oh great! Page three I hope.
Becki	Stop interrupting with your stupid jokes.
	I want to hear this bit.
Jaz	That's right! Go on, Tom.
Tom	'It is my lady, O it is my love.
	O that she knew she were.
	She speaks, yet she says nothing . . .'
Seth	That's just like the girls here.
	They're always speaking,
	but saying nothing.
	He's good this Shakespeare.
Kate	That's the last time. Just shut up, will you!
Becki	Yes, you're so immature!
Seth	All right, all right, it was only a joke.

Kate	Well just keep them to yourself.
	Carry on, Tom. You're doing really well.
Tom	'See how she leans her cheek
	upon her hand.
	O that I were a glove upon that
	hand,
	That I might touch that cheek.'
Becki	Oh that's nice, I like that bit.
Kate	So do I. Sexy, isn't it?
	Come on, Becki. It's your turn.
Becki	Oh is it me? '. . . Ay me.'
Tom	'She speaks.
	O speak again, bright angel . . .'
Becki	'O Romeo, Romeo, wherefore . . .'
Tom	Hey, wait a minute! I haven't finished yet.
Becki	You just told me to speak again, so I did.
Tom	But I've got all this other stuff first.
Jaz	Oh forget about that, that's boring.
	You carry on, Becki.
Becki	'O Romeo, Romeo, wherefore art
	thou Romeo?'
Seth	He's behind you!
Kate	Look, will you shut up!
	Besides, it doesn't mean that.

Seth	What do you mean?
	She says, 'Where are you, Romeo?'
Kate	No she doesn't. She says,
	'Wherefore art thou Romeo?'
	Not 'Where are you, Romeo?'
Seth	What's the difference?
Kate	She's talking about names.
	She means, 'Why is your name Romeo?'
	Look, she carries on and says . . .
Becki	'Deny thy father, and refuse thy name,
	Or if thou wilt not, be but sworn
	my love,
	And I'll no longer be a Capulet.'
Kate	She's saying, 'Don't be a Romeo anymore,
	and if you say you love me, I won't be a
	Capulet.'
Jaz	So names don't matter.
Kate	Exactly! See, she carries on . . .
Becki	'What's in a name? That which
	we call a rose
	By any other name would smell
	as sweet.'
Kate	So a rose would still be a rose
	whatever you called it,
	and Romeo would still be Romeo
	whatever his name was.

Seth   Yes, she's right too.
　　　　Tom would smell just the same
　　　　whatever he was called. Awful!

groans all round

　　　　All right, that's the last, I promise.
Becki But why is Juliet so hung up on names in
　　　　any case?
Kate   Because that's what it's all about.
　　　　That's why they're fighting.
　　　　It's two families with different names,
　　　　and they hate each other.
Jaz   Is that all?
　　　　All this fighting and death,
　　　　just because they've got different names?
　　　　That's not very likely, is it?
Kate   I think it's dead right.
　　　　I mean, you think of all the killing
　　　　in the world.
　　　　Isn't most of it just different names,
　　　　or different colour, or different religion?

Seth	You're right, Kate. Maybe there is something in this Shakespeare after all.

the bell rings

	But we'll just have to wait till next lesson to find out.

The class packs up, and goes out.
Last to go is **Tom**. **Becki** *waits for him.*

Becki	(*shyly*) Tom?
Tom	Yes?
Becki	You read that really well.
Tom	Oh thanks.
Becki	I didn't know you could read poetry like that.
Tom	Well, I just spoke it, you know . . .
Becki	It was all full of feeling. It sounded really nice.
Tom	Well, it was nothing special.

Becki   Yes it was.

*She takes hold of his hand,
and smiles at him.*

You can read me some more poetry if you want.

She lets him go, and goes out.

Tom   *looks surprised, and then grins to himself*
I think Seth was right.
There is something in this Shakespeare after all.

He goes out